A SHORT HISTORY OF THE
NATIONAL PARKS
BRIEF STORIES OF AMERICA'S BIGGEST LANDSCAPES
THE SOUTHEAST

WILL C. DE MAN

Will C. De Man

To my wife

Who reignited my love for the national parks

Contents

INTRODUCTION

For spring break 2022, my wife and I packed our dog into our vintage camper van and embarked for Mammoth Cave National Park. We were traveling seven hours south from our home in Michigan, and we hoped that we would get blessed with warm weather and a fun adventure. We got one of those things, and it wasn't the warm weather.

To escape the rainy Kentucky April weather, I perused the bookstore, hoping to find something to tell me more about the park. I wanted to know who first found the cave and what their experiences had been. I wanted to know about the indigenous cultures of the region and how they interacted with the cave. I wanted to know who first began developing the area for tourism. I wanted to know who had first advocated for it to be preserved as a public park.

Over the next several months, my wife and I visited eight national parks in the southwest. At each one, I continued my search, hoping for a history guidebook to teach me more about the parks. There simply was nothing like it—and that is why I wrote this book.

When I was fourteen years old, my family embarked on the All-American Road Trip. We packed our camper, crammed five kids into the back of an SUV, and took off for the American West. We saw Badlands, Yellowstone, the Tetons, and the Black Canyon of the Gunnison. This is the type of book that I would have wanted on that trip.

Since that childhood adventure, I've felt a draw to the wide open expanses of America's public lands. The call is constant, beckoning me away from email notifications and work responsibilities. The call promises peace, an opportunity for body, mind, and soul to be restored. It carries an invitation to return to a timeless human experience, a communing with nature.

This book is full of similar stories. Stories of people who feel drawn to the ancient and wild lands of this country. Stories of people who find comfort and rest on mountaintops and islands. It's a communal experience that the modern national park traveler can share with all those who came before them.

The ability to escape from our loud and rapid-fire normalities is one of the reasons why we even have parks in the east. A primary motivation to establish Shenandoah and Great Smoky Mountains National Parks were their proximity to large, urban population centers. With just a day's drive, you could leave behind the hum and grime of New York, Detroit, Chicago, or Pittsburgh, and find yourself listening to birdsong, breathing in the clean mountain air.

For some, this retreat to nature is a way to find healing. From Stephen Mather at Hot Springs to Herbert Hoover at Shenandoah, the parks of the east provide a sort of public therapy. The parks are like medicine, clearing the congestion of our minds and the pain of our hearts. While the common notion may be that mankind has saved the parks, in reality, perhaps it is the parks that save us.

This book is intended to add to whatever journey you may be on. If you want to know the history of the parks, you will find plenty of facts and information here. If you love the natural world and are inspired by champions of conservation, this is their story. And if you're looking for healing in the natural world, you will find solidarity.

"There is merit for all of us in the ancient tale of the giant Antaeus, who every time he touched his mother earth, arose with strength renewed a hundredfold."

Franklin Delano Roosevelt

HOT SPRINGS
NATIONAL PARK - ARKANSAS

Hot Springs is one of the most unique areas in the National Park System. Most national parks preserve landscapes by setting aside the most astounding and captivating vistas in the country. The landscape of Hot Springs is mountainous yet pleasant. It possesses unique springs but not dramatic geysers, and attracts many tourists for its spa-town luxuries rather than its wilderness appeal. People do not travel here to experience a rugged connection to nature, but rather to relax in one of nature's gifts.

Unlike the hot springs and mud pots of Yellowstone National Park, the hot springs of Arkansas are not volcanic in nature. Instead, the water seeps through the ground following faults beneath the Ouachita Mountains. Over the course of several thousand years, water finds its way further and further into the earth, naturally heating as it goes. The water will then run into a fault line and return to the surface. This natural cycle happens due to the unique geology of the region and takes approximately 4,400 years in total to occur.

In 1803, what is now Arkansas was purchased from France by the United States. At the time of the Louisiana Purchase, the Hot Springs region was inhabited primarily by the Quapaw people. How exactly the Quapaw and other Native Americans may have interacted with the springs is unknown, but medicinal purposes are likely.[1] A novaculite mine in the region reveals their knowledge of and presence in Hot Springs 3,000 years ago.[2]

In 1818, a treaty was made with the Quapaw to cede Hot Springs to the United States. Both William Clark and Meriweather Lewis, of the famed transcontinental expedition, had a hand in the ratification of the treaty.[3] One of the defining hallmarks of the region is the conflict over control of its natural resources. This treaty could be viewed as the first in a series of Hot Springs land disputes.

In 1820, just two years after the United States claimed the hot springs region, the Arkansas Territorial Legislature requested government protection of the site. Congress failed to take action, resulting in private land claims made in and around the springs. In this period of limited medical knowledge, the minerals found in the thermal pools were considered to be a potential cure for a variety of illnesses. Many settlers came to the area hoping that a soak in the spring would cure them of rheumatism, syphilis, and alcoholism. Though they had no real claim to the area, these bathers set up ramshackle shelters and built pools around the springs.[4]

In 1832, the territory of Arkansas sought money to establish a hospital at Hot Springs.[5] In the spring of the same year, Congress approved a law setting aside Hot Springs "for the future disposal of the United States."[6] This legislation is the beginning of Hot Springs's life as a national park. Despite being established as a reserve by the federal government, squatters and private developers continued to loiter in the region for the next four decades.

Late in the Civil War, Hot Springs was partially destroyed by an invasion of federal troops. As the town was slowly rebuilt, a lawless, wild-west aesthetic took hold. The town was overrun with gambling, prostitution, and illegal use of the federally protected pools. Squatters erected shacks and tents on the hillside, around and over the pools. Many of these illegal bathers had a legitimate need for the healing waters. They suffered greatly and did not possess the means to pay for entrance to the expensive bath houses constructed by local entrepreneurs.

The federal government recognized the lawless abuse of the publicly protected waters. Determined to make a stand against the illegal use of the pools, the Department of the Interior took four men to court over land claims. The Hot Springs Cases were settled by the Supreme Court in 1875, re-establishing federal control of the reserve.[7]

While this was a victory for the Department of the Interior, it was not the end of the conflict over land use. The first superintendent of the reserve, Benjamin Kelley, would continue to battle with the squatters and their ramshackle spa houses.[8] Many patrons illegally used the pools to soothe the excruciating neuralgia caused by syphilis. Their community became collectively known as Ral City.

Fig. 1.1: Ral City and some of its residents, 1870. Deluxe Studio. Courtesy of the National Park Service History Collection.

Kelley harnessed an 1878 fire as the opportunity to rid Hot Springs of Ral City, destroying its structures and clearing out its residents. Ral City did not go quietly. The residents rose up in revolt against Kelley, requiring the superintendent to request federal troops from Little Rock to keep the peace.[9]

The residents of Ral City claimed that they were in legitimate need of the mineral-infused waters. They were truly ill and couldn't afford to use the ornate establishments of Bathhouse Row. Instead of again attempting to remove the squatters from Hot Springs, Kelley chose compassion. He determined that Hot Springs needed to have a free bathhouse, a place where the poor and feeble could come for relief.[10] In doing so, he echoed the sentiment of the Arkansas Territorial Legislature that sought to establish a hospital at Hot Springs.[11] In December 1878, Congress passed a law guaranteeing the presence of a free bathhouse for the poor.

While the free bathhouse was intended to be open to people of all races and genders, African Americans were the exception. In the bathing facilities where they were allowed, African Americans were only given access at the least desirable times of day. They were also required to be ill to use some bathhouses, unable to soak in the springs simply for pleasure. In 1904, the Crystal Bath House was built for the specific purpose of providing African Americans with an exclusive place to bathe. The Crystal burned down in 1913, but it was replaced in 1914 by the Pythian Bathhouse. The Pythian operated successfully until the need for a bathhouse to serve African American patrons slowly faded after the Civil Rights movement desegregated public spaces.[12]

In the following decades, Hot Springs continued to develop as a retreat for rich and poor alike. Land was added to the reserve at several points, and roads and trails were built for tourists to enjoy. Though it suffered from several fires, Bathhouse Row was built with ornate spas and became the economic engine of the region. In the early 1900s, baseball teams including the Chicago Cubs and Boston Red Sox held their spring training at Hot Springs. William Jennings Bryan, a three-time presidential candidate, frequently brought his wife to the reserve where she was successfully treated for rheumatism.[13]

Fig. 1.2: Women soaking their feet in Corn Hole Spring, 1930s. Deluxe Studio. Courtesy of the National Park Service History Collection.

The most important person to visit Hot Springs Reserve was the one who would advocate for its re-designation as a national park. In 1915, Stephen Mather and his close friend and assistant, Horace Albright, visited Hot Springs for the first time. During the trip, Mather became deeply enamored with the site and began making plans for its improvement.[14] According to Albright, Mather was "addicted" to the waters and the spa treatments that accompanied them. In 1916, when the National Park Service was formed, Mather was appointed its first director.

Horace Albright's papers reveal that Mather suffered from bipolar disorder, with his manic episodes often triggered by high stress. Just after his appointment to the National Park Service, Mather suffered from one such manic-depressive period. During a previous episode, Mather's doctor had suggested his friends and family "keep him thinking about his greatest interest, national parks, but without having to make any decisions."[15] Mather was moved to Hot Springs for several months to recover.[16] Perhaps the warm, mineral-rich waters added to Mather's love of the place that could produce such a healing effect.

After his recovery at Hot Springs, Mather returned as director of the infant Park Service. He recognized that Hot Springs was a tourism powerhouse, a valuable feature for any of the early national parks. The energetic and exuberant Mather advocated for the gentle thermal pools to join the explosive geysers of Yellowstone as a national treasure. On March 4, 1921, Hot Springs was upgraded from a reserve to a national park. Mather's relationship with the park represents a unique function of many national parks—they are places where we are drawn to the healing that only nature can provide.

Fig. 1.3: National Park Service Director Stephen T. Mather feeding a chipmunk in Yellowstone National Park. Image courtesy of the U.S. National Park Service History Collection.

GREAT SMOKY MOUNTAINS
NATIONAL PARK - TENNESSEE & NORTH CAROLINA

A fter suffering from a health crisis and alcohol abuse, Horace Kephart knew that something in his life needed to change. In 1904, Kephart believed that only the mountains could save him. He left the comforts of civilization, marching into the Smoky Mountains with only a gun, a fishing rod, and three days' rations.[1] Kephart, like many people, understood the mystical call of the Great Smoky Mountains, and would become an advocate for their establishment as a national park.

Several hundred years before Kephart, the Cherokee Nation made a living in the valleys and hollows of the southern range of the Appalachian Mountains. They spread throughout the middle-south, establishing settlements on the southern and western slopes of the Smokies. Their capital, Echota, was located just southwest of the present-day park.[2] The Cherokee hunted, grew crops, and created a political system that was essentially democracy. This way of life was disrupted with the arrival of European fur traders and settlers.

As conservationist and author Michael Frome states, "The Smoky Mountains are the stories of the Eastern Cherokee, whose soul has never died, and of the back-country settlers who live on the brink of yesterday and tomorrow."[3] Two centuries before the national park's appropriation, Scotch-Irish and German settlers were scratching out a living from the mountain hollows and valley coves. The expeditions of men like Daniel Boone and William Bartram, who forged a way through the Appalachian Mountains, made a wave of settlement possible. Through the turn of the nineteenth century, Euro-Americans were stealing land from the Cherokee. This practice sparked violence and was only stopped when land claims were made legal by an 1819 treaty.

This treaty and many others were attempts to eradicate Native Americans from their homelands. Removal had many motivations but can be synthesized into one idea: white men coveted Indigenous resources. John Ross was the political leader of the Cherokee, and he lobbied in Washington, D.C. for the Cherokee to remain in their homeland. He was ultimately unsuccessful. The 1835 Treaty of New Echota forced the Cherokee out of Tennessee and Georgia and onto the deadly march known as the Trail of Tears. Only the Eastern Band of the Cherokee remained, placed on a reservation that borders the present-day park.

In the years between the Trail of Tears and the creation of Great Smoky Mountains National Park, white settlers inhabited the highlands. The Smoky Mountains were remote, and many settlers simply passed through on their way to the western plains. Those that stayed cleared small plots and built small cabins, making use of whatever flat land could be found in the hollows and coves. These communities were closely tied by kinship bonds—newlyweds sometimes moved in with their parents after marriage.[4]

By 1901, the Smoky Mountains were one of the few places left in the Eastern United States that harbored primeval forests—vast tracts of hardwoods that had never been felled or extracted.[5] As desirable lumber like Black Walnut became rare, logging companies began to turn their eyes toward the remote slopes of the Southern Appalachians. The advancement of sawmill and steam engine technology made the Smokies accessible to logging, leading to an attempt to "denude [the] mountains without mercy."[6] Timber companies began buying tracts of land in the future parkland. Champion Fibre Company owned one-fifth of the present-day park, including Clingmans Dome.[7]

Fig. 2.1: *The massive stump of a primeval tulip poplar, cut by the Little River Lumber Company. Jim Shelton, 1916. Courtesy of the U.S. National Park Service History Collection.*

A forest reserve was the original plan for preservation in the Smoky Mountains. Gifford Pinchot, a hero of the conservation movement and first chief of the United States Forest Service, supported the idea. The state legislatures of Tennessee and North Carolina, as well as the federal government, all recognized the value in practicing forestry in the Southern Appalachians. Unfortunately, the lumber lobby was strong and legislation failed to pass that would have protected the area.[8]

The first campaign for a park coincided with petitions for a forest reserve. Tourism in Asheville, North Carolina, prompted its congressional delegation to introduce a park bill in 1893.[9] Dr. Chase Ambler, an Ohio physician, moved his practice to Asheville, convinced that the Smokies were an ideal place for a medical practice. He organized the Appalachian National Park Association, which appealed to Congress for a protective designation.

While the initial movement for a park failed, the idea was not forgotten. The conservation movement was only just beginning and would be strengthened by the 1906 Antiquities Act. The Antiquities Act gave the president power to designate national monuments, protecting sensitive ecological, historical, and cultural sites from plunder and degradation. In 1916, the National Park Service was founded, further boosting campaigns to protect areas of wonder throughout the country.

Originally, the purpose of the Park Service was to preserve areas of scenic splendor for public enjoyment. This was the guiding philosophy behind the establishment of

parks in the west, each of which preserved nearly inde-
scribable vistas. The natural resources of the east simply could not compare. While advocates did identify the
scenery of the region, the preservation of the Smokies was
intricately tied to the preservation of primeval forest. The
establishment of the national park represented a slight
shift in philosophy: environmentalism was now part of the
park-making equation.[10]

One of those credited with beginning the second movement for a park in the Smokies was Anne Davis. Considered to be the mother of the park, Davis famously asked
the rhetorical question, "Why not a park in the east?"[11]
Davis was elected to the Tennessee State House of Representatives in 1924. Her first act was to introduce a bill
to preserve the Smoky Mountains as a park. This level of
bold action and advocacy is especially remarkable consid-
ering women had only gained the right to participate in
the political process with the passage of the Nineteenth
Amendment in 1919.

Anne Davis worked with her husband and others to
establish the Great Smoky Mountains Conservation Association. The association was composed primarily of local
community members in Tennessee and North Carolina,
but also included the voices of national interests. One
of these national interests was the growing automobile
industry. Thanks to the innovation of the assembly line,
personal automobiles were becoming cheaper and widely
accessible. The auto industry joined forces with the national parks movement, making the case that the personal

vehicle was the best way to see the country's great out-doors. The Great Smoky Mountains were a mere one-day drive from the biggest cities in the nation.[12]

In order to determine the best location for a park, a survey was conducted in 1924 of several locations in the southern Appalachians. The Smoky Mountains were determined to be the best, with Shenandoah's Blue Ridge earning a close second place.[13] On February 21, 1925, Congress passed "an act to provide for the securing of lands in the southern Appalachian Mountains and in the Mammoth Cave regions of Kentucky for perpetual preservations as national parks." This bill did not establish the parks, but it did allow for the process to begin. Unlike the western parks carved out of the public domain, the parks in the east would have to go through a long, complicated land acquisition process.

The primary issue in the acquisition of land was the sheer cost of it. Tennessee and North Carolina bore the responsibility of raising funds to buy the parkland. The amount of land that needed to be purchased was huge, and most of it was owned by timber companies and speculators. Speculators purchased small family tracts from the Appalachian settlers and attempted to sell it as parkland for an exorbitant price. Timber companies often refused to sell their land outright, and state governments had to exercise the power of eminent domain to condemn the land. Condemnation proceedings were costly both in time and money, and slowed the park creation process.[14]

The total sum needed to purchase the parkland was estimated at $10 million.[15] Neither North Carolina nor Tennessee could raise the money single-handedly, and the federal government was legally bound to only accept parkland as a donation. (Franklin Delano Roosevelt did find a legal loophole that allowed more than $1 million to be diverted to the project from Civilian Conservation Corps funds.) Both states engaged in mass fundraising campaigns, including the passage of bonds. Monetary and land donations came in from rich and poor alike, including $1,391.72 donated by the schoolchildren of Knoxville, Tennessee.[16] All in all, the two states could only raise $5 million—not enough to save the last best example of primeval forest from the lumberman's axe.

Like a knight in shining armor, a wealthy businessman rescued the park project and donated the remaining $5 million. John D. Rockefeller, Jr., a benefactor of the Standard Oil fortune, was a friend of Horace Albright and Arno Cammerer, both of whom helped lead the National Park Service. Rockefeller contributed to eleven national parks, including Acadia and Yellowstone. He promised to fill in the funds necessary to purchase the parkland for the Great Smoky Mountains National Park. The donation would come from a memorial fund created by his father in honor of his late wife, Laura Spelman Rockefeller.[17]

Fig. 2.2: John D. Rockefeller, Jr., who donated funds to many national park causes. Courtesy of the U.S. National Park Service History Collection.

On June 15, 1934, the federal government took control of the land that was purchased for the park. One of the stipulations of Rockefeller's donation was that a monument be erected to commemorate his mother. It stands on the border of North Carolina and Tennessee and reads,

"For the permanent enjoyment of the people. This park was given one-half by the peoples and states of North Carolina and Tennessee and by the United States of America, and one half in memory of Laura Spelman Rockefeller... by her husband John D. Rockefeller."

As Michael Frome writes, the preservation of the Smoky Mountains represents an incredible act of democracy. As a country, we decided that the rugged landscape and ancient forests of the Southern Appalachians must be protected. As a people, the states of Tennessee and North Carolina led the charge in advocacy and fundraising. As individuals, the likes of Horace Kephart, Anne Davis, and John D. Rockefeller, Jr., came together beneath a common cause. Thousands of voices across multiple decades agreed that the Smoky Mountains ought to be kept for future generations as a park in the east.

Fig. 2.3: *A historic photo of Chimney Tops, by Laura Thorn-burgh. Courtesy of the U.S. National Park Service History Collection.*

SHENANDOAH
NATIONAL PARK - VIRGINIA

When Americans think about our nation's national parks, they often imagine the rugged beauty of the West, envisioning the red rock of the Southwest and snow-capped Rockies. While the glories of wilderness are certainly a central aspect of America's public lands, many parks have deeply human pasts. Though it has in many ways been erased, the human story of Shenandoah National Park is central to the geography of the region. From the native people who originally called it home to the mountain people who were jettisoned to acquire the parkland, the history of humans in the Blue Ridge is intricately connected to the origin of the park.

One of these groups is the Souian-speaking Monacan people. The Monacan were like many native groups of the eastern United States. They maintained a complex social order, rotated their crops to keep their fields fertile, and buried their dead in large mound structures. Unlike their Algonquin-speaking neighbors on the Virginia coast, the Monacan tried to avoid contact with Europeans.[1]

Despite this self-imposed isolation, the Monacan suffered from the spread of European diseases, notably smallpox, brought by Spanish explorers to Florida. Weakened by disease, the Monacan began to assimilate with other, similarly weakened tribes. By the 1700s, the Monacan had intermingled significantly with the Tuscarora and the Cayuga, two of the five tribes that made up the Iroquois Confederacy. The majority of this Monacan-Iroquois group stayed in the Shenandoah region, where they were eventually forced into contact with European colonists.

The Anglo-American settlement of Shenandoah is another aspect of its human past. During the early 1700s, the Virginia colony began to turn its gaze westward beyond the Blue Ridge Mountains. The lieutenant governor of Virginia, Alexander Spotswood, led an expedition in 1716 across the mountains into the Shenandoah. Spotswood is credited to some degree with being the first European to cross into the Shenandoah Valley.[2] He brought with him the specific intent to expand the colony of Virginia into the western region.

In 1722, it was agreed that the Shenandoah Valley and Blue Ridge Mountains would form a buffer between the British colonies and the Iroquois, who used the valley as a warpath.[3] Despite leading settlers into Shenandoah in 1716, Spotswood agreed to halt Anglo-American settlement across the mountains. Like all treaties made between Native Americans and white people, this agreement was broken and the valley was claimed by settlers from the east.

European colonists traveled east from tideland Virginia and south from Pennsylvania. They claimed plots along the mountain passes, clearing homesteads in the dense hollows. Many of these mountain settlers lived a subsistence lifestyle, growing just enough food to survive through the winter. Some supplemented their income by working on the large plantation fields in the valley itself.[4]

These plantations were worked primarily by enslaved Africans. Like the rest of Virginia and the south, slavery was integral to the economy of the Shenandoah Valley and grew alongside it. In 1785, the Belle family plantation enslaved seventeen Africans. Thirty-five years later, farms owned by the Hite family enslaved more than one hundred humans.[5]

A key part of the slave economy of Shenandoah was the practice of hiring out surplus enslaved labor.[6] Shenandoah did not produce the cash crops typical throughout the south, such as sugar and tobacco. Because of this, slaves not needed on the farm were leased to plantations deeper in the south. This practice simultaneously built the wealth of the farmers of Shenandoah and further dehumanized the men and women they owned as property.

From the antebellum period on, Shenandoah's history continues to follow the broader narrative of American history. Shenandoah was used by Stonewall Jackson during the Civil War to tie up and confuse a large portion of the Union Army.[7] After the Civil War, slavery ended in Shenandoah and the economy began to change. As the nation industrialized, the mountain people, who had relied on their subsistence lifestyle and supplemental work in the valley, began to move out of the mountains in search of industrial jobs. Between 1900 and the establishment of the park in 1935, the population of the future parkland dwindled from 6,000 to 2,250.[8]

One resident of the future park was George Freeman Pollock. Pollock's vision, showmanship, and advocacy began the movement to establish Shenandoah National Park. In the mid-1800s, a series of vacation resorts were constructed in the Blue Ridge Mountains, serving as a retreat for the residents of large eastern cities.[9] In 1888, Pollock convinced his father and other investors to turn the copper mine they owned into a resort, calling it Skyland. Pollock was a talented entertainer and he attracted many wealthy patrons to his highland playground. He organized plays, dances, bonfires, and excursions into the Shenandoah wilderness to bring in wealthy vacationers.[10]

By the early 1900s, Pollock began to promote Shenandoah's establishment as a national park. He was not the only individual to put forth the idea. The Appalachian Trail was planned to run along the Shenandoah ridgeline, and many of the national trail system's supporters joined Pollock's call for action. Chambers of Commerce were heavily involved, organizing Shenandoah Valley, Inc., to argue for regional economic benefits.[11] In 1924, Secretary of the Interior Hubert Work began requesting recommendations for national parks in the east.[12] Shenandoah was the first place surveyed as a potential park in the Appalachian Mountains.

Fig. 3.1: *The cabins at Skyland, photo taken by George or Addie Pollock, 1912. Courtesy of the U.S. National Park Service.*

In 1925, Congress approved a bill allowing for the recommendation of park boundaries. The land acquisition process could also begin, but with one major requirement—the federal government would not purchase any land for the park. All land to be preserved would have to be donated. This created a major hurdle in the process of codifying the park, stretching it over the course of ten years. Will Carson, chairman of the Virginia State Commission on Conservation and Development, navigated all of these challenges, slowly acquiring the land deeds needed for the park.

In 1928, Virginia passed the National Park Condemnation Act, allowing it to use the power of eminent domain to force the mountain people out of their homes and claim their land. The legality of this law was challenged, further complicating the quest to acquire the land for the park. Ultimately, the law was upheld and 3,000 individual tracts of land were condemned and seized for the park. Five hundred families were forced off the land their ancestors had subsisted on for two hundred years.

As the park establishment process labored on, many people were drawn by the growing resort culture that George Pollock had cultivated. Will Carson recognized the strategic value of the president being counted among park advocates. When President Herbert Hoover requested a fishing camp be built for him as a place of retreat, Carson suggested a location on the Rapidan River, within the proposed boundaries of Shenandoah National Park.[13]

Fig.3.2: *Herbert Hoover's fishing lodge on the Rapidan. Dale Smith, 1974. Courtesy of the U.S. National Park Service History Collection.*

President Hoover and his wife fell in love with the Blue Ridge and became personally invested in the national park. Recognizing the needs of the mountain children, Hoover and his wife established Hoover Mountain School. The president rode on horseback with National Park Service director Horace Albright, planning park infrastructure. While he could have been helping rescue the country from the Great Depression, Hoover made suggestions and approved plans for Skyline Drive, considered to be one of the park's best features.[14] Shenandoah clearly provided Hoover with a place of solace and peace; perhaps it was also an escape from his progressively unpopular administration.

On December 26, 1935, Shenandoah National Park was the third park to be established in the east. The hope was that it would somehow live up to the vast wilderness areas of the west. In order to actualize this desire, the remnants of human civilization had to be covered and buried.[15] The title to more than 175,000 acres of land was transferred from the state of Virginia to the federal government. On much of this land stood the homes and barns that had served the now-removed mountain people. The Civilian Conservation Corps was tasked with removing these remains of human settlement, replacing them with natural flora. In this act, Shenandoah's human past was erased, hidden behind a facade of wilderness.

Fig 3.3: A car passes through Mary's Rock Tunnel on Skyline Drive in 1937. Courtesy of the U.S. National Park Service History Collection.

Fig. 3.4: President Hoover fly fishing in Shenandoah National Park. Courtesy of the U.S. National Park Service.

MAMMOTH CAVE
NATIONAL PARK - KENTUCKY

T he spaces beneath the surface of the earth have always fascinated and enticed us, so it is fitting that the largest known cave system in the world is preserved as a national park. The mystical allure of subterranean exploration, as well its many resources and oddities, have drawn humans to Mammoth Cave for 5,000 years.

Mammoth Cave is located in a *karst* landscape, which is defined by the presence of water-permeable stone through which water seeps and forms sinkholes and caverns. The creation of Mammoth Cave is connected to the Green River flowing through the Mammoth Cave National Park. As the river cut a valley through the hilly Kentucky terrain, the cave system grew. The cave is in reality a hollowed-out hill formed by water seeping through the limestone to join the Green River. Sinkholes in the hillside show where this water found and cut its way through the rock, creating the massive passageways and caverns that define the world's longest cave.

Mammoth Cave was first discovered through these sinkholes. Legend claims that a hunter stumbled upon Mammoth Cave late in the 18th century, becoming the first

Anglo-American to enter it.[1] Whether or not this is true, the cave was well known locally by the early 19th century. As locals began exploring the cave, they discovered undeniable evidence of an ancient Native American presence: torches made of reeds and moccasins woven from plant fibers.[2]

The mummified remains of Native Americans have been discovered throughout the karst region. A fully-clothed body, complete with jewelry, was found in Short Cave, not far from Mammoth. The mummified remains of this woman, dubbed the "Fawn Hoof Mummy" on account of her jewelry, were used as a tourist attraction to bring people to Mammoth Cave.[3] Another mummy was discovered in 1935 by members of the Civilian Conservation Corp and nicknamed "Lost John."[4]

When rediscovered by Anglo-Americans, Mammoth Cave was used in a wide variety of ways. Sodium nitrate was mined from the cave during the War of 1812, helping to supply saltpeter for the production of gunpowder. In the mid-1800s, Kentucky locals took advantage of the consistently warm temperature in the cave and used it as a Methodist chapel.

Famously, the physician Dr. John Croghan attempted to establish a hospital for tuberculosis patients.[5] It was believed that the subterranean climate and atmosphere would aid in the healing of the respiratory disease, and small huts were built inside the cave to accommodate patients. This experiment quickly failed as the health of the patients often declined rapidly after moving into the cave.

In 1838, the land on top of Mammoth Cave was purchased by Franklin Gorin and A. A. Harvey, who intended to profit off the cave as a tourist destination. Gorin's fledgling cave-guiding operation used enslaved men as tour guides.

Fig. 4.2: *Housing for tuberculosis patients, far from the sunlight in Mammoth Cave. A.V. Oldham, c. 1912. Courtesy of the Library of Congress.*

One of the enslaved was Stephen Bishop, who has a legacy as one of Mammoth Cave's most important explorers.[6] Bishop worked for the majority of his time under Dr. Croghan, who bought the land from Gorin. The land would remain in Croghan's estate until its establishment as a national park.

Bishop continued to guide tours in Mammoth Cave under Dr. Croghan and was recognized by many as extremely intelligent.[7] He was self-taught in geology and drew maps of the cave from memory. Bishop often put on a show and led adventurous tourists into unknown parts of the cave, hoping to receive tips from them as payment. In his spare time, he scoured records and surveys of the cave system and plunged solo into its depths. Bishop discovered many of the sites that visitors enjoy now and was the first to cross the Bottomless Pit. His reputation was well known, and one visitor remarked that "he seems more like the high priest and expounder of [Mammoth Cave's] mysteries than a hired guide, much less a slave."[8]

Fig. 4.2: Portrait of the legendary Mammoth Cave Guide, Stephen Bishop, 1882. Courtesy of the Library of Congress.

As early as 1901, calls started for the establishment of Mammoth Cave as a national park. In an undated text titled A *Privilege—a Duty—an Opportunity for Kentucky*, one advocate stated that "many tourists will remain in Kentucky as permanent residents and investors" and that "the money spent to secure Kentucky's National Park will be but a small investment compared to the enormous returns."[9] At the turn of the century, the cave country of Kentucky was experiencing a tourist frenzy. Nearby cave systems competed with each other for tourist dollars. Mammoth Cave and others gained national attention when cave guide Floyd Collins was trapped in Sand Cave and died after nineteen days.[10] Though tragic, this event pushed ahead the argument for the protection of Mammoth Cave.

In 1924, the Mammoth Cave National Park Association (MCNPA) was formed to promote establishment of the park. This organization included business leaders, politicians, and representatives from across the state of Kentucky who were present at its first meeting on October 7.[11] The MCNPA claimed that preservation of the park was urgent, comparing it to Niagara Falls, which had been fully claimed by consumerism and business development. In 1925, the president of the association wrote Secretary of the Interior Hubert Work saying, "Niagara Falls and the Mammoth Cave in Kentucky should both have been claimed by the National as too important scenically to have passed into private hands."[12] If Mammoth Cave wasn't set aside, it would soon become a tourist trap.

In 1926, along with the Great Smoky Mountains and Shenandoah parks, Mammoth Cave National Park was au-

thorized. Both the Mammoth Cave National Park Association and the state of Kentucky committed to raising funds
necessary to purchase the minimum 45,000 acres for the
park.[13] Purchasing the most crucial land—the estate of
Dr. John Croghan—where the cave proper was located,
proved to be extremely difficult. Croghan's heirs were not
willing to part with the property until Kentucky opted to
use the power of eminent domain.[14] On May 22, 1936, all
land acquired for the park was turned over to the National
Park Service. On July 1, 1941 Mammoth Cave National Park
was officially established.

Throughout the 20th century, cave exploration in the
surrounding area intensified. In 1972, an expedition led by
John Wilcox began in the Flint Cave System near Mammoth Cave. After six days of traveling through the "wild"
unknown cave, the leader of the expedition stumbled
upon a handrail for tourists—he had found his way into
Mammoth Cave.[15] By connecting the Flint and Mammoth
caves, Mammoth Cave grew to a total of 144 mapped miles,
establishing it as the longest cave in the world. To this day,
around 400 miles of Mammoth Cave have been mapped
and explored.

EVERGLADES
NATIONAL PARK - FLORIDA

The incredible landscape of South Florida has gone by many names. The nimble, canoe-equipped Indigenous people referred to it as "Pa-hay-okee," the grassy waters. The iron-clad Spanish explorers, unable to penetrate its depths, called it *El Laguno del Espirito Sancto*, meaning the Swamp of the Holy Spirit. A 1905 story in *The Century* dubbed it a "water wilderness."[1] In 1947, Marjory Stoneman Douglas famously referred to it as a "river of grass" and poetically described the landscape as "one word and yet plural."[2] The term "everglades" refers to its seemingly eternal expanse of saw grass, a prairie that terminates into the horizon. This phrase first appeared in 1823 and can be attributed to a surveyor named Charles Vignoles. The variety of names given to the ecosystem reveals the complexity of the human relationship with the Everglades. To some, it is a swamp in need of draining and containment. To others, it is a mystical place that should be saved at any cost.

Compared to many of the natural wonders preserved by the National Park Service, the Everglades are relatively young. Geologists believe that they formed only five to six thousand years ago. The ecosystem is defined by the sheet flow of water over the course of a hundred miles. South Florida is nearly flat with an extremely gradual elevation change, resulting in water just barely flowing out of the Lake Okeechobee region toward the Atlantic Ocean. This gradual movement of water allows for a diverse ecosystem found nowhere else on earth. Douglas described the Everglades as "unique in the simplicity, the diversity, the related harmony of the forms of life they enclose. The miracle of the light pours over the green and brown expanse of saw grass and of water, shining and slow-moving below."[3]

Archeologists have discovered considerable evidence pointing to Indigenous occupation prior to the arrival of Europeans in the 16th century.[4] Approximately 20,000 people lived in the Everglades region, and 193 archeological sites have been discovered within the national park boundary alone. These people are known broadly as the Glades cultures and subsisted as hunters and fishermen. Uniquely, the Glades cultures developed a complex political and social order, a rarity for non-agricultural societies.

These native ways of living were unavoidably disrupted by the arrival of the Spanish in the 16th century. In 1513, Ponce de Leon was the first European to explore Florida, and he did not receive a warm welcome.[5] It's likely that the Indigenous people of Florida had heard of Spanish conquest and enslavement on the Caribbean islands. The Calusa and Tequesta people of Florida responded to Spanish imperialism and evangelism by raiding forts and missions.[6] Indigenous resistance to colonization was largely successful; Ponce de Leon died from an infected wound he received in battle with natives, and Spanish colonization floundered until the 1560s.

Throughout the following centuries, South Florida experienced little colonization and development. Despite this, the population of the area changed dramatically, especially among the Indigenous groups. Florida became a haven for fragmented Native American tribes and enslaved Africans escaping from Georgia and the Carolinas. These refugee groups combined to form the Seminole people. The United States Army fought with the Seminoles several times throughout the 19th century, diminishing their population and driving them deeper into the Everglades and Big Cypress Swamp.

Around the time of the Seminole Wars, developers began turning their eyes toward the Everglades. The few white settlers who tried to make a living in South Florida stayed on the higher ground of the eastern side of the peninsula.[7] An 1848 survey and report claimed that the Everglades could be drained at a relatively minor cost and transitioned to lucrative agricultural land. In 1850, President Millard Fillmore signed the "Swamp and Overflowed Lands Act," transferring control of South Florida wetlands to the state of Florida. The Everglades could now be parceled, sold, and developed.

By the mid 1880s, through construction of canals and levees intended to drain the swamplands, the water level of Lake Okeechobee sank below the Everglades and Big Cypress Swamp. After two disastrous hurricanes in 1926 and 1928, federal and state governments were highly in-centivized to further drain and control the waters of South Florida. Levees were built, rivers were dredged, and canals were constructed, all with the aim of preventing future floods and emptying out the vast wetland.[8]

Fig. 5.1: Travelers on the Tamiami Trail. Burgert Brothers Photographer, 1923. Courtesy of the Library of Congress.

In addition, the Tamiami Trail (a road between the metro areas of Tampa and Miami) was constructed through the Everglades, effectively forming a dam. Both the drainage work and the road effectively halted the sheet flow of water through the swampland. The vital life force of the ecosystem had been forcefully placed on hiatus. Marjory Stoneman Douglas described how this ecological break affected the Everglades:[9]

"The surface of the great lake that had been so arbitrarily lowered... The lower Glades suffered. The land along the

[canals] *dried and sank in deeper and wider valleys. Where there had been the flow of the river of grass, there were only drying pools and mosquitoes.*

The saw grass dried, rustling like paper. Garfish, thick in the pools where there had been watercourses, ate all the other fish, and died and stank in their thousands. The birds flew over and far south, searching for fresh water. The lower pools shrank and were brackish. Deer and racoons traveled far, losing their fear of houses and people in their increasing thirst.

The fires began.

... Men watching from fire towers got tired of counting smokes against which they could do nothing. There was no water in the canals with which to fight them. Houses, trees, groves, were burned."

In the early years of the 20th century, many voices began to raise the idea of a national park in the Everglades. In 1905, the popular monthly magazine *The Century* published an article describing the mystery and intrigue of the region and alluding to its worthiness as a member of the National Park system.[10] Its author stated, "the mystery is part of our national inheritance... It has its place among the country's native wonders, like the Mammoth Cave... the Yellowstone and Yosemite and the [Grand Canyon] of the Colorado."

In 1916, Royal Palm State Park was established by the work of May Mann Jennings and the Florida Federation of Women's Clubs. Royal Palm was the predecessor of an Everglades National Park in two ways: It was the first attempt at preservation in the region, setting aside a massive hammock for public enjoyment; and it was also developed with a lodge and picnic areas, demonstrating that the Everglades could be made suitable for tourism.[11]

Just as Jennings had been a champion for a state park in the Everglades, many individuals would rise to argue in favor of a national park. Ruth Bryan Owens, daughter of political superstar William Jennings Bryan, represented a South Florida district in the House of Representatives and was instrumental in the passage of the Everglades park bill.[12] Ernest F. Coe, a landscape architect from Connecticut, founded the Everglades National Park Association. He conducted an extensive study of the marshlands and sent a proposal to Stephen Mather, director of the National Park Service, in spring of 1928. Coe was welcomed by the NPS and given a desk in their Washington, DC offices.

In 1930, the National Park Service conducted an official survey of the Everglades, evaluating it for a national park designation. Horace Albright, director of the NPS in 1930, wrote, "We hired a dirigible from which we got a much better view...Then we chartered a houseboat—complete with a motorboat and a canoe—to explore the land and rivers. The tropical plant life, the birds, alligators, snakes, and other wildlife fascinated everyone."[13] With a unanimous recommendation from the survey committee, Secretary of the Interior Ray Lyman Wilbur sent a report to Congress in December 1930, officially recommending creation of Everglades National Park.[14]

On a second survey of the proposed parkland, Frederick Law Olmstead, Jr. and William Wharton were struck by the vast, untouched expanse of the Everglades. It was wilderness through and through, "literally trackless and uninhabitable."[15] To many involved in the movement, this was the primary reason to preserve the Everglades. It was a unique environment untrammeled by man, deserving of protection for its sheer ecological value.

While there was a strong desire to establish more parks in the East, some conservationists believed that national park status deserved a high barrier to entry.[16] Parks needed to have significant resources worth protecting, and most important among these was a stunning vista. Yosemite, Crater Lake, and Mt. Rainer were unequivocally beautiful, and any eastern park had to meet this standard of beauty. Establishment of the Everglades and Great Smoky Mountains parks changed this perspective and added a new criteria for national park status—regions of incredible ecological rarity deserved to be preserved.[17]

Though public and private organizations alike supported the Everglades park, the bill authorizing it struggled to pass through Congress.[18] In the early 1930s, the Great Depression gripped the country and House Republicans were uncertain about adding another responsibility to the cash-strapped federal government. The bill only passed because of an amendment assuring that federal spending in the Everglades would be banned for five years.[19] On May 30, 1934, Everglades National Park was signed into law by

Franklin Delano Roosevelt. It was officially established on December 6, 1947.

While legislation for the park is mostly typical, it does have two important sections related to the specific nature of the Everglades. Olmsted's journey through the interior wilds of the Everglades had left a lasting impression on him and on many other conservationists.[20] Section 4 was added to the park bill as a result, stating, "Area or areas shall be permanently protected as a wilderness, and no development of the project or plan for the entertainment of visitors shall be undertaken."

In addition to recognition of the wilderness character of the Everglades, the bill also recognized the presence of Indigenous people in the park. Secretary of the Interior Harold Ickes and Bureau of Indian Affairs Chief John Collier were both sympathetic toward the Seminoles.

Fig. 5.2: A Seminole village on the Tamiami Trail. George A. Grant. Courtesy of the U.S. National Park Service History Collection.

Several reserves had been made in and around the Everglades to allow the Seminoles to continue their traditional living. Additionally, the Seminoles had begun to contribute to Everglades tourism by establishing villages where visitors could witness their cultural practices and customs. Though controversial, Ickes and Collier pushed for an addition to section 3 of the park bill,[21] stating that "nothing in this Act shall be construed to lessen any existing rights of the Seminole Indian which are not in conflict with the purposes for which the Everglades National Park is created."

The establishment of Everglades National Park represents the evolution of the national park idea. The "river of grass" gave birth to the modern notion of what a national park is supposed to be. While parks are places of extraordinary beauty, that is not *all* they are. National parks are places where heritage is preserved—heritage that belongs to the forces of nature, the animals that inhabit it, the first people who knew it, and the future generations who will enjoy it.

Fig. 5.3: A view of the Everglades from above. Courtesy of the U.S. National Park Service History Collection. Accessed March 2023.

BISCAYNE
NATIONAL PARK - FLORIDA

P airs of national parks exist across the United States that have bonds of landscape, ecosystem, and tourism. Zion and Bryce Canyon exist in symbiosis, Sequoia and Kings Canyon share a border, and Grand Teton was originally considered as an addition to Yellowstone. The Everglades and Biscayne National Park are another pair of associated parks. Both were established to preserve unique environments, and both have been threatened by commercial and industrial development. They both represent landscapes that, if not preserved, will disappear from the earth.

Like the Everglades, Biscayne contains considerable evidence of pre-Columbian habitation. One estimate suggests that the pre-contact population of Florida was around 350,000, with approximately one-third of those people living in the southern part of the peninsula.[1] The primary indicators of the Glades culture around Biscayne are middens—small archeological sites containing shells, potsherds, and other prehistoric trash.

The accidental discovery of middens revealed what may be the most important archeological site in the region.

Though it is not included within the boundaries of the national park, the Miami Circle can be directly tied to its Native American heritage. Attributed to the Tequesta, it is at least 2,000 years old and was likely part of a larger village complex on the Miami River, which flows into Biscayne Bay.[2] The Miami Circle is carved into limestone bedrock, with multiple, post-hole-like points chiseled around its perimeter. Though they are uncertain of its use, archeologists have determined that it was a structural footprint and may have held ceremonial importance.[3]

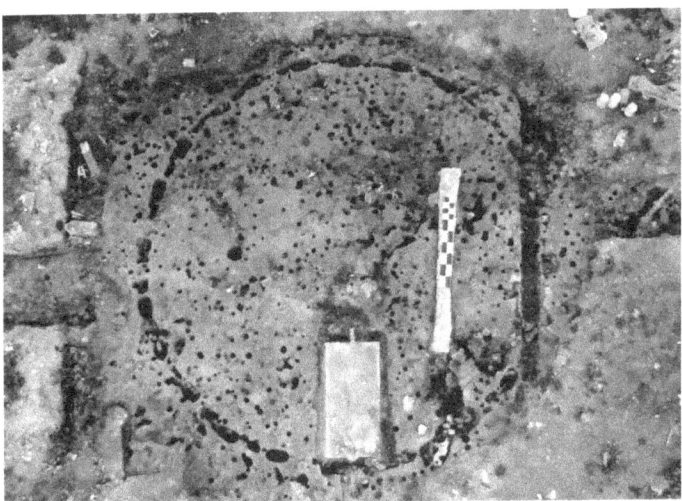

Fig. 6.1: The footprint of the Miami Circle. Florida Department of State, Historical Resources Division.

Within the park itself, several islands in the northern keys reveal pre-Columbian native inhabitants. Several middens have been discovered on Sands Key, where people likely lived from around 1,000 CE to the period of Spanish exploration and colonization. It is suspected that more archeological sites exist on the outer reefs and beneath the waters of the bay itself.[4]

European contact with natives often resulted in hostility and death. Though they prevented extensive colonization, the Tequesta and others suffered greatly from European contact. Like Indigenous people throughout North America, the population of South Florida was destroyed by disease. English reports from the 1770s describe the Tequesta villages as completely deserted.[5]

As New Spain developed in the Caribbean and Central America, the Spanish needed a trade route to transport plundered treasures back to Europe. Their vessels traveled through the Straits of Florida, using the warm Gulf Stream as a maritime highway.[6] This journey along the Florida Keys—between Cuba, the Bahamas, and the Florida peninsula—could be very dangerous. Storms shipwrecked many vessels, and some survivors were reportedly picked off by hostile natives.[7]

In 1821, Spain ceded the Florida territory to the United States. At the time, South Florida was sparsely settled. A series of wars between the United States and the Seminoles further disrupted settlement in the Biscayne region.[8] The 1830 census of South Florida records that only 517 people inhabited the area.

While very few people were migrating to South Florida, Biscayne Bay was an important destination for enslaved Africans seeking freedom.[9] Like the Underground Railroad to the North, the Saltwater Railroad was a route for enslaved people to escape to the British Bahamas.

Bahamian ships and Seminole canoes would transport people from the tip of Key Biscayne, just north of the present-day park boundary. It is estimated that between 100 and 300 formerly enslaved people escaped bondage via Biscayne.[10]

In addition to shipwrecks, castaways, and freedom seekers, Biscayne Bay attracted lawless fugitives. One legend tells of an African American pirate, Black Caesar, who established a hideout within the bay. While textual evidence is lacking, the geography of Biscayne Bay keeps the story alive—Caesar's Creek is located on Elliott Key, and some have searched there for buried treasure.[11] Black Caesar may be a villain of myth, but a real American scoundrel did briefly foray into Biscayne's crystalline waters. The former Confederate Secretary of War, John C. Breckenridge, passed through the bay on his way to exile in Cuba on June 7, 1865.[12]

Other than these renegades, Biscayne Bay received very little attention until the early 1900s. Attempts were made to produce agricultural goods on the keys, primarily pineapples and limes.[13] Elliot Key produced the second greatest quantity of pineapples in the Florida Keys, and a small town was established to support economic activity. While the region did produce a significant amount of citrus fruit, Biscayne and Miami would not boom until the arrival of the railroad.

If conservationists are the heroes of Biscayne National Park, then Henry Flagler may be one of its villains. Flagler came to Florida in winter 1878 on doctor's orders;

his wife suffered from tuberculosis and was prescribed warm ocean air. Flagler found Florida to be pleasant but completely lacking in infrastructure.[14] When the city of Miami was incorporated in 1896, it was accessible only by boat.[15] After the death of his wife, Flager started a flurry of development including extending a rail line all the way to Key West and building hotels in Miami. Others followed suit, dredging the bay to build artificial islands like Miami Beach. In the 1922-1926 land boom, both the population and the price of land in the region exploded.[16] Private estates, hotels, and fishing clubs were developed in and around the present-day park.

Fig. 6.2: A view of Miami from above Biscayne Bay, 1936. Courtesy of the U.S. National Park Service History Collection.

To develop the area, Flagler and others altered and destroyed cultural and ecological resources. The railroad to Key West required the destruction of acres of mangrove forests along Florida's east coast. The bay was cut into and dredged, opening it to sea travel and enlarging the keys.[17] A Tequesta burial mound was destroyed by Flagler to build the extravagant Royal Palm Hotel on the Miami River.[18] The rapids on the Miami River itself were blown up with dynamite to help drain the Everglades located just west of the rapidly developing city.

This destructive development impacted the broader environment. The ecosystem of Biscayne Bay is closely connected with the Everglades. The sheet flow of water that defines the river of grass mixes with the saltwater of the bay.[19] The estuary formed by this confluence of fresh and salt water creates a fertile ecosystem, one that was heavily disrupted by the draining of the Everglades and the development of Miami. Ernest Coe, a leading advocate of Everglades National Park, recognized this intricate connection and shared risk if it was destroyed. In his original plans for the Everglades park, he included Biscayne Bay.[20]

After World War II, Biscayne Bay would face two great development threats: Islandia and Seadade. The City of Islandia was incorporated in 1961 by a small group of landowners and developers on the keys ringing the bay. Islandia developers attempted to mimic the growth of Miami Beach by dredging the bay to build artificial islands and linking the keys to the mainland via automobile causeways.[21] Ultra-wealthy businessman Daniel Ludwig proposed the construction of Seadade, an oil refinery and deep-water channel to allow for industrial shipping. The majority of Biscayne Bay is extremely shallow, so a channel suitable for industrial shipping would represent a dramatic alteration of the bay floor.[22]

Both the commercial and industrial development of Biscayne Bay represented an environmental apocalypse. The combined threats of pollution, oil spills, and the catastrophic destruction of the bay-bottom inspired multiple grassroots efforts to save the bay. In the 1960s, environmentalism and conservationism were given new life by the publication of Rachel Carson's *Silent Spring*.[23] This groundbreaking text outlined the threat that chemicals and development posed to wildlife, ecosystems, and humanity itself. These threats were a clear and present danger in Biscayne Bay, and Carson's message is sure to have motivated organizers and advocates.

The grassroots effort eventually led to state and national attention for the park movement. Dante Fascell represented Miami in the U.S. House of the Representatives and deserves enormous credit for the preservation of Biscayne Bay.[24] Joe Browder, who worked with the National Audubon Society, spoke highly of Fascell, saying, "It was a really tremendous effort and there are good reasons why the visitor center at Biscayne is named after Dante. [He's] the one who really did the Bay. The rest of us—I always worked hard, but Dante is the one who really did it."[25] Along with Fascell, Secretary of the Interior Stewart Udall supported the park idea, drafting legislation and halting oil refinery permits.[26]

Stewart Udall declared his support for a national monument in Biscayne Bay in 1964. Because the monument could not be created out of federally-owned lands, congressional approval was necessary. In the proposal for the monument, National Park Service Director George Hartzog, Jr., wrote, "Without preservation and effective management, intensive private development will greatly alter existing values of the area." He laid out the purpose of the park clearly, stating that "proposals for causeways, deep water channels, real estate, and industrial developments are immediate threats to natural features." He continued, "Only by bringing these resources into public ownership will they be protected and preserved adequately and permanently for public use and enjoyment."[27]

Though the issue divided park advocates and pro-industry members of Congress, the bill to preserve the bay ultimately passed. On October 18, 1968, Biscayne National Monument was created, preserving 96,300 acres of land. Over the next decade, the borders of the monument would be extended to the north to include additional islands and to the south to make it contiguous with John Pennekamp Coral Reef State Park. In 1980, shifts in the political atmosphere allowed for the re-designation of Biscayne as a national park. At present, Biscayne National Park preserves 173,000 acres, ninety-five percent of which are underwater.

Fig. 6.3: National Park Service director George Hartzog, Jr., fishing. Courtesy of the U.S. National Park
Service History Collection.

DRY TORTUGAS
NATIONAL PARK - FLORIDA

The eight islands of the Dry Tortugas lie seventy miles beyond Key West, making it the most remote national park in the lower forty-eight states. This extreme geography makes Dry Tortugas both vitally important and hopelessly desolate. It was considered an important strategic location for a fort, yet many thought the sand was too unstable to support large-scale architecture. It provides vital dry land to migratory birds, yet it completely lacks fresh water. It is both abundant and lacking, full of wonder and also desperation.

The name "Dry Tortugas" perfectly illustrates this contradiction of resources. The Spanish first came across the islands in 1513. Hernando de Escalante Fontaneda was a Spanish sailor shipwrecked in the Florida Keys who lived among Indigenous people for nearly two decades. He described them as "the Islands of the Tortugas; for turtle are there, and many come at night to lay their eggs in the sand."[1] The adjective "dry" was added so that ships passing through the Straits of Florida knew what to expect— they would not be able to restock their water supply on these islands. In the Dry Tortugas, turtles were abundant but water was lacking.[2]

This lack of water explains why there are no known prehistoric sites on the Dry Tortugas. Indigenous people inhabited the Florida Keys to the east, but no remnant of inhabitants has been discovered on the Dry Tortugas themselves. It is entirely possible that prehistoric people knew about and used the islands 10,000-12,000 years ago, and that their archeological remains have been covered by the rising sea.[3] The oldest artifact discovered on the islands is a British cannon cast in 1700.[4]

The Dry Tortugas were claimed by the Spanish and would lapse in and out of their possession. Geopolitical conflicts such as the Seven Years War and the American War for Independence would cause the Dry Tortugas to change hands as control of Florida was passed between Spain and Britain. In 1819, the Adams-Onis Treaty finally placed Florida under the control of the United States.

As the young United States proved itself on an international scale, it became apparent that a strong coastal defense was necessary for national security. President James Madison appointed a Board of Engineers for Seacoast Fortifications to study the issue. The Board released a report in 1821 suggesting a series of fortifications from Maine to Texas, ending in the Dry Tortugas. The islands were considered to be an ideal geographic location for a U.S. military base, protecting trade along the Straits of Florida and projecting American strength toward the Caribbean and Central America. Both Commodore David Porter in

1822 and Commodore John Rodgers in 1829 confirmed the strategic value of Dry Tortugas. Both also raised concern about a lack of fresh water and potential structural issues caused by the sandy soil.[5]

When Florida achieved statehood in 1845, it deeded control of its offshore islands to the federal government. On September 17, 1845, Dry Tortugas was declared a military reserve by President James K. Polk.[6] The construction of a fort began on Garden Key in 1846. The stronghold was planned as a massive, hexagonal establishment with three tiers of guns. Built out of concrete and masonry, this fifty-foot high fortress would collect fresh water in deep underground cisterns. It would be a "mammoth"-sized fortification, capable of protecting the shipping industry, proclaiming American authority, and defending against foreign enemies.[7] It would be the "Gibraltar of America."

Fig. 7.1: An aerial view of Fort Jefferson in the Dry Tortugas. Jack E. Boucher, courtesy of the U.S. National Park Service History Collection.

Initially, the construction work was performed by white laborers who struggled in the extreme environment. It was soon determined that forced labor was the most efficient way to build the fort. Enslaved Africans were accustomed to the heat and immune to tropical diseases due to childhood exposure. The project, dubbed Fort Jefferson in 1850, would have struggled to progress without this coerced labor.[8]

Like in the Southern states, enslavers in the Florida Keys lived with a constant paranoia of slave uprisings. Due to their remoteness, the Dry Tortugas were considered to be a safe place to lease enslaved laborers. Residents of Key West sent the people they claimed as property to work on the islands, collecting a twenty-dollar monthly fee and feeling assured that their "investment" was secure. Despite the perceived safety of the Dry Tortugas, uprisings of enslaved people did occur. In the summer of 1847, a handful of enslaved laborers stole multiple schooners and attempted to escape the island, presumably intending to take refuge with the Seminoles in the Everglades. The self-emancipated escapees disabled three of the four boats they captured and embarked towards freedom in the fourth. When the escape attempt was discovered, several boats from multiple islands took part in the manhunt. The freedom seekers were ultimately captured and forced back into bondage.[9]

In the early years of construction, the process was slow and very little was accomplished. Despite the strategic value of the fort, Congress appropriated very little money each fiscal year for its construction until 1856. In that year, tensions with Spain were on the rise and Fort Jefferson was recognized as vitally important for projecting strength into the Caribbean. This catalyst allowed for the rate of construction to increase. By September of 1858, the first tier of the fort had been completed and armed with cannons.[10]

While a war with Spain wouldn't materialize until 1898, the American Civil War would have a dramatic impact on the history of the Dry Tortugas and Fort Jefferson. Florida seceded from the Union on January 10, 1861, but the Dry Tortugas remained in the Union. The islands were owned and operated by the federal government and military. Fort Jefferson was one of only three forts in the South to be manned by the Union Army for the entirety of the Civil War.[11]

As the war progressed, Fort Jefferson transitioned from the Gibraltar of the Americas to the Alcatraz of the Caribbean. The use of Fort Jefferson as a prison signaled its lack of purpose as an important military installation. Midway through the Civil War, improvements in military technology rendered the fort obsolete as a weapon of war. Its strategic importance in the Union blockade of the Confederacy would be further eroded by Union victories at Vicksburg and Gettysburg in the summer of 1863.[12] Union soldiers who mutinied against their superior officers were often sent to the Dry Tortugas, whose population reached 882 prisoners in November of 1864.[13] These prisoners were often put to work on the fort construction, which still wasn't finished eighteen years after it was started.

The most famous prisoner at Fort Jefferson was Dr. Samuel Mudd, a conspirator involved in the plot to assassinate president Abraham Lincoln. Along with three other conspirators, Dr. Mudd was delivered to Fort Jefferson in July 1865, just three months after the president was murdered. Like other prisoners, Mudd was put to work in the fort, employing his medical expertise in the infirmary. Mudd treated prisoners, soldiers, and workers for the variety of illnesses that plagued the Dry Tortugas. Chief among them was dengue fever, which created a "bone-breaking" pain, and the highly feared yellow fever. Only a few months after his incarceration at Fort Jefferson, Mudd attempted to escape. The doctor tried to hide beneath loose boards on a ship leaving Garden Key. His attempt was unsuccessful and resulted in greater security measures on the island, including not allowing prisoners to leave the walls of the fort.[14] Mudd and the other conspirators would be pardoned and released by President Andrew Johnson in 1869.

Fort Jefferson was never completed after the Civil War and was eventually abandoned. As military obsolescence loomed, some began to realize a new value to the Dry Tortugas as a scientific outpost. In the early days of Fort Jefferson, Dr. Joseph Holder was sent to the Dry Tortugas to act as both a physician for the workers and a marine biologist. He was sponsored by the Smithsonian Institution and later helped establish the American Museum of

Natural History. When he wasn't tending Fort Jefferson's infirm, Holder sailed the keys, studying the coral of the Florida Reef.[15]

Fig. 7.2: The unfinished walls of Fort Jefferson. George A. Grant. Courtesy of the U.S. National Park Service History Collection.

In addition to being an important coral habitat, the islands of the Dry Tortugas are vital to migrating birds. In the spring of 1890, W.E.D. Scott performed a two-month study of the birds in the Dry Tortugas. He recorded more than eighty species, many of which were land birds stopping on the keys during their spring migration.[16] It is now known that approximately 300 species of bird pass through the Tortugas in the spring and fall, using it to recoup their strength before continuing their journey. The sooty tern and magnificent frigatebird are the only bird species that actually make a home on the Dry Tortugas.[17] When writing about Bird Key Scott remarked, "here the different Gulls and Terns breed in myriads, those which are ground nesters finding room between and *under* the bushes in which the [Noddies] build countless nests." In 1908, the Dry Tortugas were transferred to the Department of Agriculture and maintained as a National Wildlife Refuge.[18]

When combined, the ecological and historical importance of the Dry Tortugas qualify it for national park status. It began as Fort Jefferson National Monument, designated on January 4, 1935 by President Franklin Delano Roosevelt. In 1992, it was re-designated as Dry Tortugas National Park, asserting its status as a location of rich history and deep ecological value.

Fig. 7.3: Sooty terns nesting on Garden Key. Phillip C. Puderer, 1937. Courtesy of the U.S. National Park Service History Collection. Accessed March 2023.

CONGAREE
NATIONAL PARK - SOUTH CAROLINA

C ongaree National Park, near Columbia, South Carolina, is an ecological remnant, a fractional reserve of an environment that used to be common. It is the last large tract of old-growth bottomland hardwood forest left in the southeastern United States. The cutting of lumber and binding of the rivers has destroyed the majority of bottomland ecosystems that used to be present throughout the South. The champion trees of Congaree, some of the tallest in the nation, stand as guardians of this now-rare ecosystem. While it possesses no majestic peaks or dramatic canyons, Congaree is the last of its kind and rightfully protected as a national park.

The Congaree River valley has been inhabited for at least 10,000 years, populated by Indigenous people who likely migrated into the floodplain from the Appalachian Mountains.[1] While Spanish explorers were the first Europeans to explore the area, they failed to establish settlements in South Carolina. Their greatest impact on the region was the introduction of Old World diseases that obliterated Indigenous cultures throughout the Americas.[2] It was the English settlers who would force out the

Native Americans of Congaree. Many poor immigrants lacked the economic ability to compete with the enslaving plantations on the South Carolina coast, so they pushed inland in search of available land. These settlers subsisted economically by raising cattle and hogs, using the Congaree and Wateree rivers to float their livestock to market.[3]

During this time, a small group of Native Americans, bearing the same name as the present-day national park, struggled to survive amidst the multiple cataclysms occurring around them. The Congaree people were dying of Old-World illnesses, fighting with other tribes, and suffering from European coercion. Just after the turn of the 18th century, the Congaree strategically moved their village to the western bank of the Congaree River, giving them better access to European trade routes.[4] This allowed the Congaree to trade deerskins with the English, who became interested in building a fort nearby.

Unfortunately for the Congaree, the pressures they faced overwhelmed them. In 1715, a significant conflict between Native Americans and English settlers erupted throughout South Carolina. This conflict, known as the Yamasee War, was caused partially by the Native American slave trade. Throughout the eastern U.S., Indigenous groups had practiced the tradition of capturing and enslaving enemies as a result of war. Prior to European contact, this practice was motivated by tradition and intended to help manage population change as a result of war. With the rise of the plantation economy, the Native American slave trade transitioned from a tradition-based practice to a profit-motivated enterprise. Many Natives had incurred large trade debts to the English, and enslaving a handful of their peers could mean freedom from financial bondage.[5]

It is known that the Congaree engaged in the slave trade, provoking the ire of neighboring tribes.[6] When the Yamasee War ended in 1717, the Congaree were one of many tribes that were essentially destroyed. Survivors assimilated with the Catawba, disappearing as a distinct Indigenous group.[7] Like the swamp itself, rare remnants of the Congaree people can be found hidden in the terrain. The mounds they built to bury their dead stand as monuments—reminders of the original people of the Congaree.[8]

Despite many attempts, white settlement and development of the Congaree Swamp was a futile endeavor. Beginning in the colonial period, land was granted to poor white settlers by either the King of England or the Royal Governor of South Carolina.[9] Though they owned the right to develop and cultivate their tracts of land, many failed to do so, leaving them untouched and abandoned. Authorities repeatedly re-parceled them and handed them over to naive hopefuls who thought they could tame the swamp.[10] The farmers who did manage to make a living in the swamp built small earthworks to counteract periodic flooding, including mounds of earth for their livestock to stand upon.

Coastal planters tried on several occasions to take advantage of the rich, swamp-fed soils of the Congaree.[11] Enslaved Africans were brought in to clear and drain the land for the production of cash crops like rice and indigo. The planters soon realized that the use of valuable enslaved labor in the disease-ridden swamp was a huge liability. In 1825, Robert Mills described the swampland saying, "what clouds of miasma, invisible to the sight, almost continually rise from these sinks of corruption, and who can calculate the extent of its pestilential influence?"[12] The economic cost of an enslaved person dying of disease was too great a risk to gain the fertile river soil.

This cycle of hope and disappointment in the Congaree Swamp continued until into the 20th century. During the Reconstruction period, the value of the Congaree swampland plummeted, reaching rock bottom at $1 an acre.[13] Francis Beidler, a Chicago developer, saw an investment opportunity in the Congaree. Through the Santee River Cypress Company, Beidler purchased 15,000 acres of the Congaree swamp, intending to cut its cypress trees for timber.

Unfortunately for Beidler, the swamp was just as rugged and unmanageable as it had proven to be for 300 years. As his men harvested cypress trees from the bottomland, they struggled to do so efficiently. Their harvesting strategy required them to float the trees down the Congaree River, but many trees proved too heavy, sinking to the bottom.[14] By 1915, the Santee River Cypress Company's books were in the red, and Beidler chose to halt timber harvesting in the swamp.[15]

Rather than sell off the land to some other fool who thought they could tame the Congaree, Francis Beidler chose to turn his holdings into a timber reserve. Perhaps, sometime in the future, it would become profitable again. This decision opened the door for a future conservation movement that would save the Congaree Swamp.

The trees of the Congaree have been referred to as the "Redwoods of the East" due to their champion status.[16] Champion trees hold a record for being the largest of their species, a determination that is made by combining their girth, height, and canopy width. The Congaree Swamp contains both state and national champion trees. It has been debated whether these Sequoia-esque specimens grew large and fast due to the fertile swamp soil, or whether they are simply ancient, like their kin in the Sierra Nevadas. Records from the Beidler lumber mill show that the average cypress harvested was between 500 and 700 years old. One primordial cypress had 1600 rings, making it a contemporary of Constantine the Great.[17]

When logging ceased in the early 1900s, people began to recognize the importance of protecting the ecological sole survivor that is the Congaree Swamp. Chief among them was Harry Hampton, a passionate outdoorsman and newspaper editor. Having formed several organizations devoted to natural resource protection in South Carolina, Hampton was described as being "always synonymous with conservation."[18] In the 1950s, Hampton began to present the idea of protecting Congaree. Hampton was a member of a hunting club that leased land in the Beidler tract and he knew the landscape extremely well. When Hampton ran into a conservation-minded colleague, he was reportedly able to produce a map of its champion trees from memory on a shopping bag.[19]

Many conservationists recognized that Harry Hampton was "the guiding force" and "backbone" to the protection of Congaree. He possessed a powerful editorial platform at *The State*, a newspaper located in Columbia, South Carolina. He used his "Woods and Waters" column to write about conservation and argue for the natural value of Congaree Swamp. In addition to making a public argument in his newspaper, Hampton lobbied members of the federal government to evaluate Congaree for protection.[20]

In 1963, the Southeast Regional Office of the National Park Service issued a report on the suitability of Congaree as a unit in the National Park system. This report recommended that Congaree Swamp be preserved as a national monument, saying, "the biological and geological attributes of the area are in themselves worthy of national recognition and all the more so since they are unique, none being presently represented in the National Park system." Of the champion trees that guard the swamp, the report declared "[they] would make a fine complement to the record trees of other species preserved in the upland forests of Great Smoky Mountains National Park."[21]

While the National Park Service favored the creation of Congaree Swamp National Monument, there was little pressure to do so quickly.[22] Active logging had all but ceased in the swamp and it was in very little immediate danger. This changed very quickly when the price of hardwood lumber spiked in 1969. The Beidler family, who still owned their 15,000-acre tract, began cutting timber in the Congaree Swamp once again.[23]

This imminent threat kickstarted the dormant movement to protect Congaree. A public awareness campaign began in the early 1970s that quickly gained support. The grassroots effort grew rapidly and was able to oppose the protests of the forestry industry, which wished to continue logging.[24] In 1975, legislators from South Carolina authored and introduced bills to Congress to establish the national monument. On October 18, 1976, Congaree Swamp National Monument was signed into law by President Gerald R. Ford.

Though the national monument had been established, the land for the park still had to be acquired. The original 1963 report stated that the Beidler Tract and five other properties along the northern bank of the Congaree River should make up the majority of the park. The Beidler Tract was estimated to have a value of more than $30 million and was acquired shortly after the legislation protecting Congaree was passed.[25]

Over the next several decades, Congaree would receive several important designations, including International Biosphere Preserve and Globally Important Bird Area. Its place in the national park system also meant that it opened up recreation opportunities for 1.5 million people within a day's drive of the park. In 2003, Congress re-designated the monument as Congaree National Park.

Fig. 8.1: *Harry Hampton beside a bald cypress in Congaree Swamp. Courtesy of the U.S. National Park Service History Collection.*

EXPERIENCE THE HISTORY

HOT SPRINGS NATIONAL PARK

- Soak in a Hot Spring
- Stroll Bath House Row
- Climb Hot Spring Mountain where Ral City was

GREAT SMOKY MOUNTAINS NATIONAL PARK

- Find Mt. Kephart on a map
- See the homes of the mountain people in Cades Cove
- View the Champion Fibre Co. tract from Clingman's Dome
- Read the Rockefeller Memorial at Newfound Gap

SHENANDOAH NATIONAL PARK

- Hike to a displaced mountain home in Nicholson hollow
- Visit the Massanutten lodge, part of Skyland
- See Herbert Hoover's camp on the Rapidan
- Tour of the overlooks of Skyline drive

MAMMOTH CAVE NATIONAL PARK

- See the saltpeter mines at the Historic Entrance
- Stand beneath the methodist preacher's pulpit
- Witness where tuberculosis was treated
- Stare down Stephen Bishop's Bottomless Pit

EXPERIENCE THE HISTORY

EVERGLADES NATIONAL PARK

- Drive down the Tamiami Trail

- Visit Royal Palm and the Ernest F. Coe Visitor Center

- Gaze across the Marjory Stoneman Douglas Wilderness

BISCAYNE NATIONAL PARK

- See the prehistoric Miami Circle (outside the park)

- Take a boat to Caesar's Creek

- Stand on Elliot Key and eat pineapple

- Visit the Dante Fascell Visitor Cetner

DRY TORTUGAS NATIONAL PARK

- Take the ferry from Key West

- Stand on the unfinished walls of Fort Jefferson

- View the cell of Dr. Samuel Mudd

CONGAREE NATIONAL PARK

- Try to wrap you arms around a champion tree

- Visit the Harry Hampton visitor center

YOUR OWN EXPERIENCES OF NPS HISTORY:

This project would not have been possible without the support, encouragement, and sacrifices of so many people. First and foremost is my wife, Mikayla. She has supported and encouraged this project from the start, allowing me to spend many evenings and weekend hours researching and writing. Without her, this book probably never would have happened. In addition, this book was fueled by the support of all my family members. In particular, my mom, Katrina, who offered many words of motivation and advice. Thanks also goes to Chris, Jay, Kristen, Kipp, Sarina, Simone, Glenn, Kristin, Hannah, Colin, Emma, Cole and Atticus for always listening to my many ideas and history facts.

I also had support from many people on the technical production of this book. Ann edited this book and helped me polish it. Landon did the initial proofread. Pete answered lots of questions. Sarina created the amazing map graphic for the cover.

And I can't forget my students, who get overly excited for "National Park Mondays" and have been asking for constant updates on the book.

Will C. De Man is a history teacher from West Michigan. He has a wife, a son named after a Great Lake and a dog named Keith. He studied history, education, and classical studies at Calvin University. He loves camping, reading, and dreaming of Sequoia trees. Will runs the Instagram account @nationalparkhistory where he shares more stories of the people, events, and places that form our public lands. You can find more from Will and sign up for his newsletter at nationalparkshistory.com.

Author's Note

I wrote this book because I love our national parks and believe in their mission. National Park Service Director George Hartzog, Jr., wrote "park philanthropy is more than money and materials; it is devoted men, women, and children contributing, selflessly, of their own time and talents. Their genius, creativity, and downright hard work enrich the park experience of every visitor."

This book is full of stories of men and women, slave and free, rich and poor, who devoted themselves to the protection of our nation's greatest wonders. By sharing their stories, you and I are able to share in their legacy.

If you want to be a part of spreading the story of our national parks, there are two things you can do. The first is to leave a review for this book on Amazon. It really does help more people see the book and support my work.

The second is to tell your friends and family about this book. If it made your park-going experience better, please share about it on your social media. If you found these stories intriguing and want more of them, please give a copy to a friend. The national parks are public land, intended for everyone to enjoy. These stories are our public history, a heritage we all should remember.

By doing these things, you and I can support the mission of the National Park Service. We can share in the legacy of Stephen Mather, Anne Davis, and Harry Hampton. We can "enrich the park experience of every visitor."

Endnotes

Hot Springs National Park

1. US Department of the Interior, National Park Service Midwest Regional Office, Hot Springs National Park. *Hot Springs National Park Cultural Resources Report and Environmental Assessment*, by Quinn Evans Architects, Mundus Bishop Design, Woolpert, Inc. January, 2010, 7.

2. Ibid., 5, 7.

3. Treaty ceding land from the Quapaw to the United States in return for payment, Quapaw-US, August 24, 1818.

4. "Uncovering Ral City (US National Park Service)." National Park Service, US Department of the Interior, last modified July 7, 2022, https://www.nps.gov/articles/000/uncovering-ral-city.htm.

5. Department of the Interior, National Park Service, *The Hot Springs of Arkansas Through the Years: A Chronology of Events*, Hot Springs, by Sharon Shugart, 2004, 8. https://npshistory.com/publications/hosp/chronology.pdf

6. Ibid., 3.

7. US Department of the Interior, National Park Service Midwest Regional Office, *The Hot Springs of Arkansas — America's First National Park*, by Ron Cockrell, 2014, 28.

8. Ibid., 45; "Uncovering Ral City (US National Park Service)".

9. US Department of the Interior, *The Hot Springs of Arkansas*, 46-50.

10. Ibid, 51; "Uncovering Ral City (US National Park Service)".

11. Thomas Cox, "From Hot Springs to Gateway: The Evolving Concept of Public Parks, 1832-1976," Environmental Review 5, no. 1 (1981): 19, https://www.jstor.org/stable/3984530

12. "African Americans in the Hot Springs Baths," National Park Service, US Department of the Interior, last modified September 9, 2021, https://www.nps.gov/articles/000/african-americans-and-the-hot-springs-baths.htm

13. U.S. Department of the Interior, *The Hot Springs of Arkansas Throughout the Years: A Chronology of Events.*

14. Horace M. Albright and Marian Albright Schenck, *Creating the National Park Service: The Missing Years*, (Norman, OK: University of Oklahoma Press, 1999) 116.

15. Horace M. Albright and Robert Cahn, *Birth of the National Park Service: The Founding Years*, 1913-33 (Salt Lake City, UT: Howe Brothers, 1985) 52.

16. Albright, *Creating the National Park Service: The Missing Years*, 314.

Great Smoky Mountains National Park

1. Wilma Dykeman and Jim Stokeland, *Highland Homeland* (Washington, D.C.: Division of Publications, National Park Service, US Department of the Interior, 1978) 133, 140.

2. Michael Frome, *Strangers in High Places*, exp. ed. (Knoxville, TN: University of Tennessee Press, 1980) 34.

3. Ibid., 9.

4. Ibid., 8.

5. Ibid., 161-162.

6. Ibid., 161.

7. ibid., 166-167.

8. Ibid., 173-177.

9. Frome, *Strangers in High Places*, 174; Theodore Catton, *A Gift For All Time: Great Smoky Mountains National Park Administrative History* (Gatlinburg, TN: Great Smoky Mountains Association and Great Smoky Mountains National Park, 2008) 12.

10. Alfred Runte, *National Parks: The American Experience*, 5th. ed. (Lanham, MD: Lyons Press, 2022) 106.

11. Catton, *A Gift for All Time*, 19; Frome, *Strangers in High Places*, 182.

12. Catton, *A Gift for All Time*, 23. Frome, *Strangers in High Places*, 182.

13. Ibid., 180-185.

14. Ibid., 194-198.

15. Horace M. Albright and Robert Cahn, *Birth of the National Park Service: The Founding Years*, 1913-33 (Salt Lake City, UT: Howe Brothers, 1985) 214.

16. Frome, *Strangers in High Places*, 189.

17. Frome, *Strangers in High Places*, 206-216; Runte, *National Parks*, 107; Albright, *The Birth of the National Parks*, 214.

Shenandoah National Park

1. The Monacan Nation, "Our History," copyright 2015, https://www.monacannation.com/our-history.html

2. US Department of the Interior, National Park Service, Shenandoah National Park, *Shenandoah National Park Historic Resource Study*, by Robinson and Associates, Inc., 1997, 6.

3. "Excerpts from the Treaty of Albany (1722)," in World History Commons, https://worldhistorycommons.org/excerpts-treaty-albany-1722 [accessed February 24, 2023]

4. U.S. Department of the Interior, *Shenandoah Historic Resource Study*, 8-12; George F. Pollock, *Skyland: The Heart of Shenandoah National Park* (Auckland, New Zealand) chap.1, Kindle.

5. US Department of the Interior, National Park Service, Northeast Regional Office, *'Stars Fought from Heaven': Race and Slavery in the Shenandoah Valley from Early Settlement to Jim Crow*, by Dr. James J. Broomall, September 2020, 2.

6. U.S. Department of the Interior, *'Stars Fought from Heaven*,' 49.

7. U.S. Department of the Interior, *Shenandoah Historic Resource Study*, 25.

8. Ibid., 8.

9. Ibid., 35-36.

10. Pollock, *Skyland*, 96, 112-136.

11. Ibid., 317-347.

12. Ibid., 317.

13. U.S. Department of the Interior, *Shenandoah Historic Resource Study*, 44.

14. Horace M. Albright and Robert Cahn, *Birth of the National Park Service: The Founding Years, 1913-33* (Salt Lake City, UT: Howe Brothers, 1985) 239; SU.S. Department of the Interior, *Shenandoah Historic Resource Study* 46.

15. Audrey J. Horning, "When Past is Present: Archeology of the Displaced in Shenandoah National Park" (paper presented at Society for Historical Archeology Conference, Long Beach, CA, January 10-14, 2001).

Mammoth Cave National Park

1. David Rains Wallace, *Mammoth Cave: Official National Park Handbook* (Washington, D.C.: US Department of the Interior, Division of Publications, Harpers Ferry Center, 1998) 12.

2. Cecil E. Goode, *World Wonder Saved: How Mammoth Cave Became a National Park* (Mammoth Cave, KY: The Mammoth Cave National Park Association, 1986) 4.

3. Wallace, *Mammoth Cave*, 13.

4. Ned J. Burns, "Preservation of the Mammoth Cave Mummy," The Regional Review 3, nos. 4 & 5, (October-November) 1938, https://www.nps.gov/parkhistory/online_books/regional_review/vol3-4-5h.htm

5. Goode, *World Wonder Saved*, 5-8.

6. Ibid., 8.

7. Ibid., 8-10; "Stephen Bishop," Mammoth Cave National Park, National Park Service, last updated March 25, 2021, https://www.nps.gov/peo ple/stephen-bishop.htm

8. Marianne Finch, *An Englishwoman's Experience in America* (London, Richard Bentley, 1853) 351, quotes in Goode, *World Wonder Saved*, 10.

9. A *Privilege— a Duty— an Opportunity for Kentucky*, 3, 8. https://archive.org/details/APrivilegeADutyAnOpportunityForKen tucky/page/n1/mode/2up

10. Australian Press Association, "Floyd Collins Body Will Not Be Disturbed," Townsville Daily Bulletin, February 19, 1925; "Tragedy at Sand Cave," Mammoth Cave National Park, National Park Service, last modified May 3, 2021, https://www.nps.gov/articles/000/tragedy-at-sand-cave.htm?utm_s ource=article&utm_medium=website&utm_campaign=experience_m ore&utm_content=large

11. Goode, *World Wonder Saved*, 22.

12. Ibid., 24,

13. Ibid., 32

14. Ibid., 32

15. Richard D. Lyons, "A Link is Found Between Two Major Cave Systems", New York Times, December 2, 1972; "Exploring the World's Longest Cave", Mammoth Cave National Park, National Park Service, last modi-fied September 7, 2022.

Everglades National Park

1. Edwin Asa Dix and John Nowry MacGonigle, ""The Everglades of Florida: A Region of Mystery," The Century, November-April, 1904-1905.

2. Marjorie Stoneman Douglas, *The Everglades: River of Grass*, (Lanham, MD: Pineapple Press, 2021), chap. 1, sec. 1, Kindle. (Originally published in 1947).

3. Ibid., chap. 1, sec. 1, Kindle.

4. US Department of the Interior, National Park Service, Everglades National Park, *Wilderness on the Edge: A History of Everglades National Park*, by Robert W. Blythe, 2015, 12-16.

5. U.S. Department of the Interior, *Wilderness on the Edge*, 17.

6. Alan Taylor, *American Colonies: The Settling of North America* (New York, NY: Penguin Group, 2001), 76-78.

7. U.S. Department of the Interior, *Wilderness on the Edge*, 28.

8. US Department of the Interior, National Park Service, Biscayne National Park, *Biscayne National Park: The History of a Unique Park on the "Edge,"* by Leslie Kemp Poole, 2021, 24.

9. Stoneman Douglas, *River of Grass*, chap. 15, Kindle.

10. Dix and MacGonigle, "The Everglades: A Region of Mystery."

11. U.S. Department of the Interior, *Wilderness on the Edge*, 51.

12. Horace M. Albright and Robert Cahn, *Birth of the National Park Service: The Founding Years, 1913-33* (Salt Lake City, UT: Howe Brothers, 1985) 257.

13. Ibid., 256.

14. U.S. Department of the Interior, *Wilderness on the Edge*, 83.

15. Alfred Runte, *National Parks: The American Experience*, 5th. ed. (Lanham, MD: Lyons Press, 2022) 121.

16. Runte, *National Parks*, 118; U.S. Department of the Interior, *Wilderness on the Edge*, 77-78; Paul Sutter, "Driven Wild: The Problem of Wilderness," Forest History Today (Spring 2002): 6.

17. Runte, *National Parks*, 120; U.S. Department of the Interior, *Wilderness on the Edge*, 78.

18. Albright, *Birth of the National Park Service*, 257-260.

19. U.S. Department of the Interior, *Wilderness on the Edge*, 93.

20. U.S. Department of the Interior, *Wilderness on the Edge*, 90.

21. Robert H. Keller and Michael F. Turek, *American Indians in the National Parks* (Tucson, AZ: University of Arizona Press, 1998) 223-227.

Biscayne National Park

1. US Department of the Interior, National Park Service, Biscayne National Park, *Biscayne National Park Ethnographic Overview and Assessment*, by John C. Russell, Manoj Shivlani, Jackson Underwood, Martin Watson, Daniel Suman, and Michael A. Downs, October 2006, sec. 2-1.

2. US Department of the Interior, National Park Service, *Miami Circle Special Resource Study*, November, 2007, 8.

3. Ibid., 5.

4. U.S. Department of the Interior, National Park Service, Biscayne National Park, *Biscayne National Park Historic Resource Study*, by Jennifer Brown Leynes and David Cullison, January 1998, 10.

5. Ibid., 10; US Department of the Interior, National Park Service, Biscayne National Park, *Biscayne National Park: The History of a Unique Park on the "Edge,"* by Leslie Kemp Poole, 2021, 5.

6. U.S. Department of the Interior, *A Park on the "Edge"*, 6.

7. John Viele, *The Florida Keys: Volume 3 - the Wreckers* (Sarasota, FL: Pineapple Press, 2001, 2011) 7, 20. Kindle.

8. U.S. Department of the Interior, *A Park on the "Edge"*, 10.

9. Margo Harakas, "Underground Railroad to the Bahamas," The Chicago Tribune, April 14, 2005; Matthew Wills, "The Saltwater Railroad," JSTOR Daily, September 6, 2019 ;U.S. Department of the Interior, *A Park on the "Edge"*, 10.

10. Harakas, "Underground Railroad to the Bahamas."

11. Alan F. Troop, "Legends of Black Caesar," South Florida Sun-Sentinel, October 6, 1991, https://www.sun-sentinel.com/news/fl-xpm-1991-1 0-06-9102090910-story.html

12. U.S. Department of the Interior, *A Park on the "Edge"*, 12.

13. U.S. Department of the Interior, *Biscayne Historic Resource Study*, 14.

14. Gail Clement "Everglades Biographies: Henry Morrison Flagler," Reclaiming the Everglades: South Florida Natural History, 1884 to 1934, http://everglades.fiu.edu/reclaim/bios/flagler.htm

15. U.S. Department of the Interior, *A Park on the "Edge"*, 18.

16. U.S. Department of the Interior, *Biscayne Historic Resources Report*, 20; U.S. Department of the Interior, *A Park on the "Edge"*, 18, 22.

17. U.S. Department of the Interior, *Biscayne Historic Resources Report*, 20, 22.

18. U.S. Department of the Interior, *A Park on the "Edge"*, 18.

19. Ibid., 18-19.

20. Ibid., 21.

21. U.S. Department of the Interior, *Biscayne Historic Resource Study*, 25; "The Birth of Biscayne National Park," National Park Service, https://www.nps.gov/bisc/learn/historyculture/the-birth-of-biscayne-national-park.htm, updated February 2, 2017.

22. US Department of the Interior, National Park Service, *Biscayne National Monument: A Proposal* (Florida, 1966). http://npshistory.com/publications/bisc/proposal/foreword.htm

23. U.S. Department of the Interior, *A Park on the "Edge,"* 41-43.

24. Ibid., 44-52

25. Joe Browder, transcript of oral history interview, December 10, 2008, box BISC 5526, "Congressman Saylor's Fishing Trip Reunion," BNP, Homestead, FL (hereafter "Browder, fishing interview") quoted in *A Park on the "Edge,"* 52.

26. U.S. Department of the Interior, *A Park on the "Edge,"* 43-44.

27. US Department of the Interior, *Biscayne National Monument.*

Dry Tortugas National Park

1. Hernando de Escalante Fontaneda, "Memoir of the things, the shore, and the Indians of Florida, to describe which, none of the many persons who have coasted that country knows how to describe it" [c. 1575], transl. Buckingham Smith. Washington, 1854.

2. US Department of the Interior, National Park Service, Southeast Regional Office, Cultural Resources Division, *Dry Tortugas National Park: Garden Key Cultural Landscape Report*, by Susan L. Hitchcock and Beth W. Byrd, June, 2011, 9.

3. Ibid., 9.

4. Thomas Reid, *America's Fortress: A History of Fort Jefferson*, Dry Tortugas, Florida (Gainesville, FL: University of Florida Press, 2006) 47.

5. Reid, *America's Fortress*, 2-4, 6, 10; U.S. Department of the Interior, *Dry Tortugas Cultural Resources Report*, 11-12.

6. U.S. Department of the Interior, *Dry Tortugas Cultural Resources Report*, 12; US Department of the Interior, National Park Service, *National Register of Historic Places Application Form: Fort Jefferson National Monument*, prepared by George T. Morrison, John Wesley Phillips, Richard A. Rasp, April, 1974.

7. Ibid.

8. Reid, *America's Fortress*, 16, 29.

9. Ibid., 16, 30; US Department of the Interior, National Park Service, Dry Tortugas National Park, *The Underground Railroad at Fort Jefferson*, https://www.nps.gov/drto/planyourvisit/upload/Underground -Railroad-1.pdf

10. U.S. Department of the Interior, *Dry Tortugas Cultural Resources Report*, 15-16.

11. US Department of the Interior, *National Register of Historic Places: Fort Jefferson National Monument*.

12. Reid, *America's Fortress*, 59-60, 68.

13. Ibid., 83.

14. Ibid., 88, 89, 96, 102-107, 111-112.

15. Ibid., 26-28.

16. W.E.D Scott "On Birds Observed at the Dry Tortugas," The Auk: A Quarterly Journal of Ornithology, vol. 7, no. 4, (October, 1890) 303-304.

17. "The View From Above," Dry Tortugas National Park News, US Department of the Interior, vol. 3, no. 1

18. "The View From Above," Dry Tortugas National Park News; Cultural Landscape Report, 173.

Congaree National Park

1. James L. Michie, *Archaeological Survey of Congaree Swamp: Cultural Resources Inventory and Assessment of a Bottomland Environment in Central South Carolina* (Columbia, South Carolina: SC Institute for Archaeology and Anthropology, 1980) 54-55.

2. Michie, *Archeological Survey of Congaree Swamp*, 61, 64;. "People of the Floodplain", NPS.gov, last updated December 6, 2023. https://www.nps.gov/cong/learn/historyculture/history-culture.htm

3. Michie, *Archeological Survey of Congaree Swamp*, 62; "People of the Floodplain".

4. James Mooney, "Siouan Tribes of the East," Bureau of American Ethnology Bulletin 22, 1894, 77-81.

5. Archaeology Month Poster - The Yamasee War: 1715 - 1717, 2015. Columbia, SC: University of South Carolina, South Carolina Institute of Archaeology and Anthropology, 2015. https://scholarcommons.sc.edu/cgi/viewcontent.cgi?article=1023&context=archmonth_poster

6. Mooney, "Siouan Tribes of the East," 79.

7. Archeology Month Poster – The Yamasee War: 1715-1717

8. John Cely, "Is the Beidler Tract Virgin?" in Congaree Swamp: Greatest Unprotected Forest on the Continent (Columbia, South Carolina: South Carolina Environmental Coalition, 1975), 91.

9. Cely, "Is the Beidler Tract Virgin?" 92.

10. Ibid., 92.

11. US Department of the Interior, National Park Service, *Historic Resources of Congaree National Park*, prepared by Jill Hanson, November 1995, 5.

12. Ibid., 5.

13. Cely, "Is the Beidler Tract Virgin?" 93.

14. Bob Janiskee, "Francis Beidler's Long-Ago Decision saved the Forest that Became Congaree National Park," National Parks Traveler, October 18, 2   0   0   8   . https://www.nationalparkstraveler.org/2008/10/francis-beidler-s-long-ago-decision-saved-forest-became-congaree-national-park

15. US Department of the Interior, National Park Service, Congaree National Park, *Congaree National Park History* https://www.nps.gov/cong/planyourvisit/upload/History.pdf; Janiskee, "Francis Beidler's Long-Ago Decision".

16. Cely, "Is the Beidler Tract Virgin?" 91.

17. Ibid., 93.

18. Tom Kapsidelis, "Colleagues Praise Conservation Record" The State, November 17, 1980. Accessed February 2, 2023,

19. Ibid.

20. Elizabeth J. Almlie, "A Place of Nature and Culture: the Founding of Congaree National Park, South Carolina," Federal History, (2011): 4, http://npshistory.com/publications/cong/fh-3-2011.pdf.

21. US Department of the Interior, National Park Service, Southeast Region, *Specific Area Report: Proposed Congaree Swamp National Monument, South Carolina* (Virginia, 1963) 1-2, http://npshistory.com/publications/cong/sar-1963.pdf

22. Almlie, "A Place of Nature and Culture," 4.

23. Janiskee, "Francis Beidler's Long-Ago Decision."

24. Almlie, "A Place of Nature and Culture," 5.

25. Lee Bandy, "Seek Congaree Preserve" The State, May 27, 1976, Accessed February 2, 2023. https://www.newspapers.com/image/7506 91285; Janiskee, "Francis Beidler's Long Ago Decision".